GIANT ISOPODS
AND OTHER
CRAFTY CRUSTACEANS

Heidi Moore

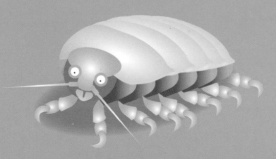

Chicago, Illinois

www.heinemannraintree.com
Visit our website to find out
more information about
Heinemann-Raintree books.

To order:
☎ Phone 888-454-2279
💻 Visit www.heinemannraintree.com
to browse our catalog and order online.

Edited by Megan Cotugno and Abby Colich
Designed by Philippa Jenkins
Picture research by Hannah Taylor
Originated by Capstone Global Library
Printed and bound in China by CTPS

15 14 13 12
10 9 8 7 6 5 4 3 2

Library of Congress Cataloging-in-Publication Data
Moore, Heidi, 1976-
Giant isopods and other crafty crustaceans / Heidi Moore.—
1st ed.
p. cm.—(Creatures of the deep)
Includes bibliographical references and index.
ISBN 978-1-4109-4198-5 (hc)—ISBN 978-1-4109-4205-0
(pb) 1. Isopoda—Juvenile literature. 2. Crustacea—Juvenile
literature. I. Title.
QL444.M34.M66 2012
595.3—dc22   2010038225

Acknowledgments
We would like to thank the following for permission to
reproduce photographs:

© Caroline Hoyoux p. 20; © Kevin Raskoff p. 28; Corbis
pp. 8 (© epa/ Raoul Wegat), 24 (© Ralph White), 27 (Tim
Rue); FLPA pp. 6 (Minden Pictures/ Piotr Naskrecki), 12
(Steve Trewhella), 13 (Nigel Cattlin), 14 (Fred Bavendam/
Minden Pictures); Getty Images p. 25 (Keystone); Image
Quest Marine pp. 9, 21 (Peter Batson); naturepl.com pp. 7, 19
(David Shale); NOAA p. 18; NOAA Ocean Explorer Gulf of
Mexico Expedition 2002 p. 15; Photolibrary pp. 10 (Oxford
Scientific/ Paul Kay), 11 (Oxford Scientific/ Per-Gunnar
Ostby); Press Association Images p. 23 (AP); Rex Features pp.
4 (Bournemouth News), 29 (KeystoneUSA-ZUMA); Science
Photo Library pp. 16, 26 (Alexis Rosenfeld); SeaPics.com p. 22
(Lia Barrett); Shutterstock p. 17 (© Chris Howey)

Cover photograph of a Giant Isopod reproduced with
permission of © Image Quest Marine.

We would like to thank Michael Bright for his invaluable help
in the preparation of this book.

Every effort has been made to contact copyright holders of
material reproduced in this book. Any omissions will be
rectified in subsequent printings if notice is given to the
publisher.

All the Internet addresses (URLs) given in this book were valid
at the time of going to press. However, due to the dynamic
nature of the Internet, some addresses may have changed, or
sites may have changed or ceased to exist since publication.
While the author and publisher regret any inconvenience this
may cause readers, no responsibility for any such changes can
be accepted by either the author or the publisher.

CONTENTS

The Mysterious Deep Sea 4

Life in the Deep Sea 6

Deep-Sea Giants 8

Crafty Crustaceans 10

Marine Isopods 12

Giant Isopods 14

Giant Eggs and Roly-Polies 16

Boiled Shrimp 18

Wood-Eating Crabs 20

Blind Lobsters, Furry Lobsters 22

Exploring the Deep Sea 24

Cool Tools 26

Saving the Deep Sea 28

Glossary 30

Find Out More 31

Index 32

Some words are printed in bold, **like this**. You can find out what they mean by looking in the glossary.

THE MYSTERIOUS DEEP SEA

In March 2010, a **submarine** was exploring the deep ocean. When it came up to the surface, scientists saw something strange. A bizarre creature was attached to the sub. The creature looked like a giant crab. It was 76.2 centimeters (2.5 feet) long, from the tip of its head to its tail. The scientists were stunned. They figured it latched onto the sub at a depth of about 2,590 meters (8,497 feet).

This is a giant isopod.

Ocean Zones

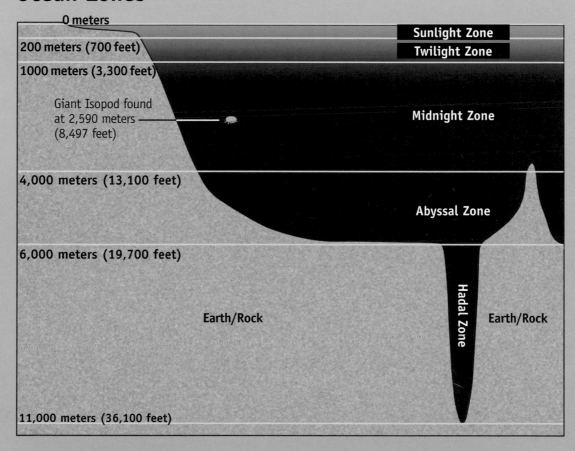

0 meters	
200 meters (700 feet)	Sunlight Zone
1000 meters (3,300 feet)	Twilight Zone
Giant Isopod found at 2,590 meters (8,497 feet)	Midnight Zone
4,000 meters (13,100 feet)	
	Abyssal Zone
6,000 meters (19,700 feet)	
Earth/Rock	Hadal Zone Earth/Rock
11,000 meters (36,100 feet)	

Giant isopods

The creature turned out to be a giant **isopod**. Some people call this creature a "monster bug." It is related to shrimp and crabs. Giant isopods live in the deep waters of the Pacific, Atlantic, and Indian oceans. Scientists know very little about giant isopods. It is difficult to study them in their deep-sea **habitat**. People need special equipment to breathe and move around deep underwater. But giant isopods are amazing creatures!

Life in the deep sea is difficult. No sunlight makes its way down there. At deep-sea depths, there is total darkness. The water is very cold. There is also intense water **pressure**. The farther below the surface, the harder it is to survive.

Monster Bugs

Some scary movies have featured giant monster bugs. A **crustacean** is not really a bug. But it has many legs like insects do. Giant crustaceans are odd-looking creatures. Sometimes people are afraid of things that look strange or unusual.

This is a giant katydid, a type of insect.

A bell jelly glows with bioluminescence.

Glowing creatures

Many deep ocean dwellers have **adapted** to this harsh **habitat**. They have unique features that help them survive there. Some creatures, such as deep-sea shrimp, make their own light. The light is given off after a special reaction takes place. The light produced by living things is called **bioluminescence**. Have you ever seen fireflies at night? They are bioluminescent, too.

Freshwater, Salt Water

Freshwater is found in lakes and rivers. It contains little salt. Seas and oceans have salt water. The word **marine** is used to describe things from the sea.

DEEP-SEA GIANTS

Some **marine** creatures have unusual features. These features help them survive far below the surface of the water. Features that creatures have developed over time that help them survive are called **adaptations**.

Gigantism

One feature is gigantism. This comes from the word *giant*. Creatures with gigantism are very large. **Crustaceans**, like the giant **isopod**, are more likely to have deep-sea gigantism.

This giant squid weighs 245 kilograms (540 pounds).

Why so large?

So what makes some creatures grow so large? Scientists have a few ideas about this. First, there are fewer **predators** in the deep sea than in other parts of the ocean. Also, animals grow very slowly in such cold water, but have very long lives. The large size then helps them control their body temperature.

Smaller creatures

Many creatures in the deep sea are tiny. This makes sense. A small size means a creature does not need much food. It is tough to find food far below the surface. Most deep-sea dwellers feed on dead animals that sink down from above.

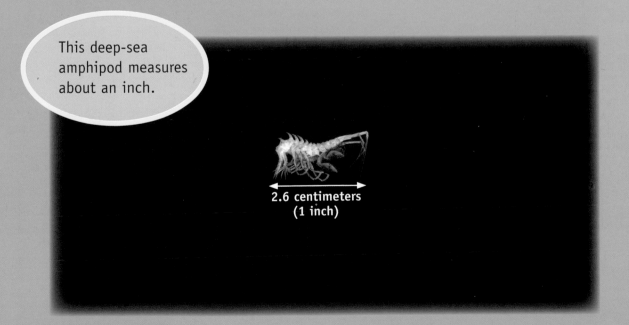

This deep-sea amphipod measures about an inch.

2.6 centimeters
(1 inch)

CRAFTY CRUSTACEANS

There are many different kinds of **crustacean**. In fact, there are about 50,000 types! Lobsters, shrimp, water fleas, tiny krill, and copepods are all types of crustaceans. Most crustaceans live in the water. Some live in freshwater **habitats**. Others live in **marine** habitats.

Different types of crustacean look very different from one another. But all share one feature: two pairs of **antennae**. They use the antennae for feeling, tasting, and smelling. Insects only have one pair of antennae.

A lobster is a type of crustacean.

Skeleton on the outside?

All crustaceans have an **exoskeleton**. An exoskeleton is a hard covering on the outside of the body. This hard covering supports and holds in the crustacean's body. (A human skeleton is on the inside.) When a crustacean grows, it molts. This means it sheds its exoskeleton. But don't worry! It grows another, larger one.

A ghost crab, a type of scavenger, feeds on a dead fish.

Finding food

Most crustaceans are **scavengers**. They feed on dead plants and animals. Some are **predators**. That means they hunt other animals for food.

MARINE ISOPODS

Marine isopods are a type of **crustacean**. The word *isopod* means "equal-footed." Marine isopods are many-legged creatures that live in the water. Most live on or near the seafloor.

Sea-slater

A common type of isopod is the sea-slater. It lives under stones and in cracks in rocks. Fully grown, it has seven pairs of legs. Sea-slaters hide during the day. At night they come out and feed on brown seaweed.

Can you count how many pairs of legs this sea slater has?

Gross!

One unusual isopod is a type of louse. It replaces the tongue of certain fish! First, it sneaks in through the fish's gills. Then it attaches to and eats away at the tongue. This tongue-eating louse will latch onto what's left of the tongue and continue to live in the fish's mouth. The fish lives on and can still eat.

Roly-Poly Relatives

Aquatic isopods are related to the wood louse, or pill bug. Some people call this a roly-poly. They can roll into a ball for self-defense. Curved into a ball, their hard **exoskeleton** protects them.

This grey garden wood louse lives in the soil.

GIANT ISOPODS

Giant **isopods** are the largest **aquatic** isopods. They live in the deep waters of all the oceans. Giant isopods are found 170 to 2,140 meters (550 to 7,020 feet) below the surface of the water. They grow up to 46 centimeters (18 inches) long.

What's for dinner?

Giant isopods are **scavengers**. This means they feed on dead animals. Giant isopods feed on the carcasses of whales and fish. This dead matter sinks down to the sea floor from above. The giant isopod's complex mouth helps it tear apart its food. Some scientists believe the giant isopod also feeds on live **sponges** and **sea cucumbers**.

Giant isopods feed on the remains of dead fish, such as this shark.

Do People Eat Giant Isopods?

It is difficult to fish for giant isopods. They live far below the surface of the water. Fishers don't cast their nets and traps that deep. And by the time the giant isopod reaches the surface, it has been scavenged by other creatures. But occasionally fishers catch a giant isopod that reaches the surface intact. It is then sold in markets and eaten in some parts of the world.

These giant isopods have been accidentally caught by fishers.

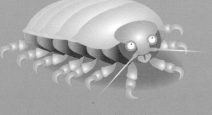

GIANT EGGS AND ROLY-POLIES

Scientists first discovered the giant **isopod** over 130 years ago. But they know very little about how giant isopods live. It is difficult to study them in their **habitat**. The deep sea is very dark and cold. People cannot survive that far underwater without special equipment.

Giant isopods have the largest eggs of any **marine invertebrate**. Invertebrates are animals without a backbone. (Humans have backbones. **Crustaceans** do not. They have **exoskeletons**.) Mother giant isopods **brood** their eggs under plates on their legs.

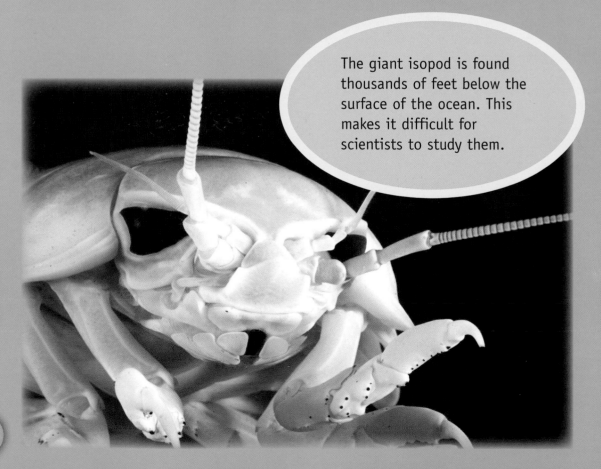

The giant isopod is found thousands of feet below the surface of the ocean. This makes it difficult for scientists to study them.

Protection from attack

When it is attacked, a giant isopod can roll itself into a ball. This is just like the pill bug, or roly-poly. The hard exoskeleton protects the giant isopod from **predators**.

Scientists

Alphonse Milne-Edwards was a French scientist. He lived from 1835 to 1900. He discovered the giant isopod in 1879. He fished a huge male isopod out of the Gulf of Mexico. People were excited about this amazing discovery. And they still are!

A pill bug rolls into a ball to protect itself from a predator, just like a giant isopod.

BOILED SHRIMP

Another type of crafty **crustacean** lives in the deep sea—shrimp. These deep-sea shrimp are very different from the shrimp you eat.

Surviving the heat

Some kinds of shrimp can survive very harsh conditions. They are found near vents that let out hot steam and liquids from deep within Earth. Temperatures near these vents are very high. The water may be boiling hot—or even hotter. In some places, the water is hot enough to melt lead!

Deep-sea shrimp cluster near a vent.

Adaptations

Other shrimp can deal with extreme cold. Some of these shrimp have very large eyes. This helps them take in what little light there is in the deep sea. Other shrimp are **bioluminescent**. They make their own light. This helps them to distract or blind **predators**.

This deep-sea shrimp has bioluminescent organs.

WOOD-EATING CRABS

Some types of crabs also have developed unusual features. These features helped them **adapt** to their deep-sea **habitat**.

One type of crab has very odd eating habits. Wood-eating crabs munch on trees and other wood pieces that have fallen to the ocean floor. They even feast on shipwrecks! Scientists found out about their strange diet by cutting apart a dead crab. They looked at the contents of its stomach. Inside its stomach was shredded wood!

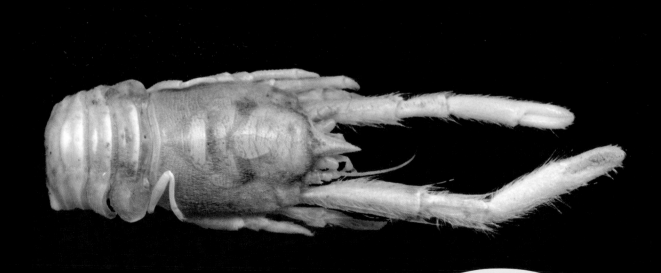

This crafty crustacean is a wood-eating crab.

Different eating habits

Eating wood is a strange behavior for a crab. Most **crustaceans** are **scavengers**. They eat dead animal matter that floats down from above. Other crustaceans are **predators**. They feed on other animals. But these wood-eating crabs eat only plant matter. Their stomachs contain **bacteria** that help them break down wood.

Crab or Lobster?

Another name for the wood-eating crab is the squat lobster. But it is not a lobster at all. It is a type of crab.

This squat lobster makes its home near a vent.

BLIND LOBSTERS, FURRY LOBSTERS

Two types of lobsters have developed very strange features. These features helped them **adapt** to life in the deep ocean.

Claws to help see

Blind lobsters cannot see. Eyes are not much help so deep below the water's surface. Little to no sunlight filters down that far. Instead, blind lobsters have very long, thin claws. They look a bit like tweezers. The claws help them find and capture food. They also help the lobsters move around on the sea floor.

The blind lobster uses its claws, not eyes, to find food.

The furry lobster is an eyeless crustacean.

A fur coat for protection

Another type of **crustacean** lives in the deep ocean. The furry crustacean has a white body covered with long hair-like strands. It lives very deep in the ocean, at about 2,300 meters (7,546 feet). The furry crustacean lives near **hydrothermal** vents. These hot vents spew out (release) steam and poisons. **Bacteria** in the crustacean's fur help it filter out poisons. This helps it survive in its harsh **habitat**. Like the blind crustaceans, furry crustaceans also cannot see. There is no light deep in the sea where they live.

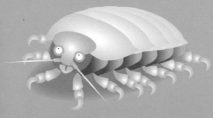

EXPLORING THE DEEP SEA

Crafty **crustaceans** have **adapted** to life in the deep ocean. Humans have not. We cannot survive for long in the deep sea. The extreme cold and **pressure** are deadly to humans.

But there are many reasons to explore the deep sea. Scientists want to learn about the amazing animals that live there. But they cannot just swim down and look around. Even a wet suit and scuba gear are not enough. To explore the deep ocean, scientists need special vehicles and equipment.

This remote viewer studies a deep-sea crab.

Scientists

Many scientists study the deep sea. **Marine biologists** focus on ocean-dwelling animals.

This early deep-sea vehicle, called a bathysphere, helped scienctists explore the deep ocean.

The bathysphere

One early deep-sea device was the bathysphere. It was a round **sphere** made of steel. Two people could fit inside. The steel held up to the intense water pressure. Inside was an oxygen tank so the people could breathe. In 1934 two scientists dove down to 923 meters (3,028 feet) below the surface. At the time, no one had been that far underwater.

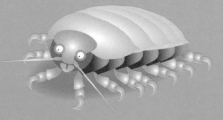

COOL TOOLS

Deep-sea devices have come a long way since the bathysphere. Today there are many cool tools that help scientists explore the ocean floor.

Small submarines

Deep-sea **submersibles** travel far underwater. They are like **submarines**, only smaller. Some submersibles stay attached to boats or submarines on the surface. Scientists fit inside and control the movement of the submersible. They explore the deep ocean and collect animal samples. Giant isopods move too fast for submersibles to catch. But they can be caught in traps.

Vehicles like this help scientists explore the deep ocean.

Scientists use ROVs to explore dangerous or very difficult-to-reach places in the ocean.

Remote control

Other tools are controlled from above. These are called ROVs, short for "remotely operated vehicles." These submarine robots move around the ocean floor, take pictures or videos, and collect samples. ROVs can access places too dangerous for humans.

SAVING THE DEEP SEA

The world's oceans are so large, it may seem like we do not need to worry about them. But we do.

Danger from people

The deep ocean is Earth's largest habitat. Today this unique habitat is in danger. **Pollution** threatens to change or harm the deep sea. Human activity has led to **global warming**. Slowly, the temperatures in the deep sea are rising. Crustaceans and other animals that are used to very cold conditions may not survive. They cannot **adapt** quickly enough to these changes.

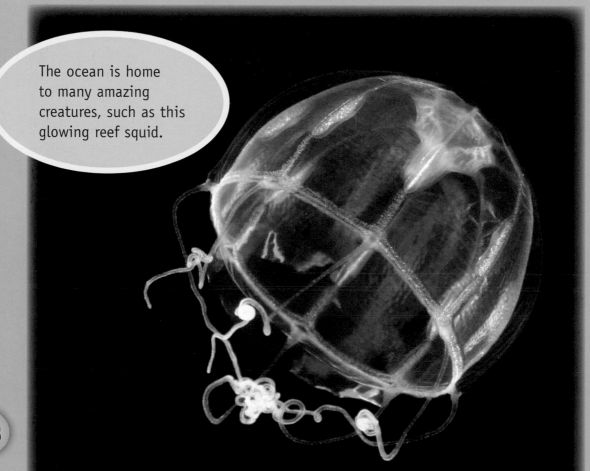

The ocean is home to many amazing creatures, such as this glowing reef squid.

Pollution, such as the oil shown here, poses a major threat to the world's oceans.

More to explore

It is important to protect the deep ocean. There is still much to learn about it. We know little about many of the amazing animals that live there. Many deep-sea dwellers have not been discovered yet. Scientists know more about the surface of the moon than the deep sea.

Final Frontier

Very few people have explored the deep sea. In fact, more people have gone into space!

GLOSSARY

adapt to change to fit an environment

adaptation feature developed over time that helps a living thing to survive in its environment

antenna (pl. antennae) sense organ on the head

aquatic having to do with water

bacterium (pl. bacteria) living thing made up of a single cell

bioluminescence light given off by a living thing

brood to grow eggs

crustacean living things with a hard exoskeleton, two pairs of antennae, and a pair of legs on each segment

exoskeleton hard outer structure on some animals

global warming rises in temperature that are taking place around the world

habitat place where a living thing lives

hydrothermal having to do with hot water

invertebrate animal without a backbone

isopod group of marine crustaceans

marine having to do with the ocean

marine biologist scientist who studies plants and animals in the ocean

pollution harmful waste

predator animal that hunts other animals

pressure force that pushes in all directions

scavenger animal that eats dead plant or animal matter

sea cucumber simple marine invertebrate with a cucumber-shaped body

sphere evenly round object like a ball

sponge simple marine invertebrate with a soft body

submarine vehicle built to operate underwater

submersible small underwater craft

FIND OUT MORE

Books

Claybourne, Anna. *Deep Oceans (Earth's Final Frontiers)*. Chicago: Heinemann Library, 2008.

Gilpin, Daniel. *Lobsters, Crabs, & Other Crustaceans. (Animal Kingdom Classification)*. Minneapolis, Minn.: Compass Point, 2006.

MacQuitty, Miranda. *Ocean. (DK Eyewitness Books)*. New York: DK Publishing, 2008.

Websites

http://kids.nationalgeographic.com/kids/activities/new/ocean
Learn about the creatures that make their home in the ocean. You can also play games and do activities.

www.seasky.org/deep-sea/giant-isopod.html
Learn more about the giant isopod at this website.

www2.scholastic.com/browse/article.jsp?id=3748096
Read about how scientists explore the deep ocean.

INDEX

adaptation 7, 8, 19, 20, 22, 24, 28
antennae 10

bacteria 21, 23
bathyspheres 25
bioluminescence 7, 19
blind lobsters 22
bodies 9, 11, 23
body temperatures 9
brooding 16

carcasses 14
claws 22
crabs 5, 20, 21

depth 4, 5, 6, 9, 14, 15, 16, 18, 19, 22, 23, 24, 25, 26

eggs 16
exoskeletons 11, 13, 16, 17
exploration 4, 24, 25, 26, 29
eyes 19, 22, 23

fishing 15
food 9, 11, 12, 14, 20, 21, 22
freshwater 7, 10
furry lobsters 23

giant isopods 4, 5, 8, 14, 15, 16, 17, 26
gigantism 8
global warming 28
Gulf of Mexico 17

habitats 5, 7, 10, 16, 18, 20, 23, 28
hydrothermal vents 18, 23

insects 6, 10, 13, 17
invertebrates 16

legs 6, 12, 16, 22
life spans 9
lobsters 10, 21, 22

marine isopods 12
Milne-Edwards, Alphonse 17
molting 11
mouths 13, 14

oxygen 25

pill bugs 13, 17
plants 11, 12, 21
pollution 28
predators 9, 11, 15, 17, 19, 21
pressure 6, 24, 25

remotely operated vehicles (ROVs) 27

salt water 7, 10
scavengers 11, 14, 15, 21
scientists 4, 5, 9, 14, 16, 17, 20, 24, 25, 26, 29
sea-slaters 12
shrimp 5, 7, 10, 18, 19
sizes 8, 9, 14
submersibles 26
sunlight 6, 16, 19, 22, 23

temperatures 6, 9, 16, 18, 19, 24, 28
tongue-eating louse 13
traps 15, 26

wood-eating crabs 20, 21
wood louse 13